Ocelot

by Grace Hansen

Abdo Kids Jumbo is an Imprint of Abdo Kids
abdobooks.com

abdobooks.com

Published by Abdo Kids, a division of ABDO, P.O. Box 398166, Minneapolis, Minnesota 55439.

Printed in the United States of America, North Mankato, Minnesota.

052022

092022

Photo Credits: Getty Images, Minden Pictures, Science Source, Shutterstock

Production Contributors: Teddy Borth, Jennie Forsberg, Grace Hansen
Design Contributors: Candice Keimig, Victoria Bates

Library of Congress Control Number: 2021950550

Publisher's Cataloging-in-Publication Data

Names: Hansen, Grace, author.

Title: Ocelot / by Grace Hansen.

Description: Minneapolis, Minnesota : Abdo Kids, 2023 | Series: South American animals | Includes online resources and index.

Identifiers: ISBN 9781098261832 (lib. bdg.) | ISBN 9781098262679 (ebook) | ISBN 9781098263096 (Read-to-Me ebook)

Subjects: LCSH: Ocelot--Juvenile literature. | Wildcat--Juvenile literature. | South America--Juvenile literature. | Rain forest animals--Juvenile literature. | Zoology--Juvenile literature.

Classification: DDC 599.7--dc23

Table of Contents

South America

South America is filled with lovely landscapes, from rain forests to mountain ranges. Because of these special places, a **diverse** group of animals live on the **continent**. Ocelots are just one of these animals.

North America
Europe
Asia
Africa
South America

Ocelots

Ocelots are wild cats found mainly in South America. However, their **range** stretches as far north as Mexico and Texas.

Ocelots like to have many safe places to hide. They live in areas with lots of plants, like rain forests.

These cats spend most of their time on the ground. But they can also swim and climb trees.

Ocelots are medium-sized cats. They can weigh up to 34 pounds (15.4 kg). From head to tail, they measure around 4 or 5 feet (1.2–1.5 m).

Ocelots have beautiful fur coats. Their fur is a golden color covered in a dark pattern. White fur covers their bellies.

Hunting

Ocelots have a good sense of smell. Their eyesight is also good. They can see very well at night. This is when they do most of their hunting.

Baby Ocelots

Ocelots are **solitary** animals. But they do come together to have young. After two months, females give birth to up to four kittens. Kittens are born with darker fur and markings.

The mother cares for and feeds her kittens. She teaches them to hunt. Kittens will stay with their mother for up to 2 years.

More Facts

- Ocelots hunt all sorts of **prey**. They mainly eat small rodents. But they will also eat birds, lizards, snakes, fish, rabbits, and other foods.

- Ocelots sleep for most of the day. They find safe spaces to sleep, like under bushes, on a tree branch, or inside a hollow tree.

- These cats can live up to 10 years in the wild. In zoos, they can live up to 20 years.

Glossary

continent – one of the earth's seven major areas of land. The continents are Africa, Antarctica, Asia, Australia, Europe, North America, and South America.

diverse – of different kinds or sorts.

prey – an animal that is hunted by other animals for food.

range – the area throughout which a living thing naturally lives or occurs.

solitary – living without others.

Index

Visit **abdokids.com** to access crafts, games, videos, and more!

Use Abdo Kids code **SOK1832** or scan this QR code!